ENDORSEMENTS

By focusing on her own experiences with various investment strategies, author Joan Hing King keeps the discussion concrete and easily understandable. She doesn't explore theories—she recounts actual real estate deals that paid off—and in some cases, continue to do so. A must read, if you are planning on investing in the real estate market. All my real estate investments have been successful! Thank you Joan.

— Margaret Hachay

It is with exceptional pride and admiration that I endorse 'The Path to Real Estate Riches : A Beginner's Guide to Creating Your Fortune through Property Investment'. A seminal work by my sister, Joan Hing King, whose passion for empowering others shines as brightly as her expertise in Real Estate Investing. Her approach is as much about nurturing confidence as it is about imparting knowledge. Joan has the rare gift of speaking to the heart as she does to the mind, guiding readers through the intricacies of property investment with the gentleness of a mentor coupled with the precision of a seasoned expert. Watching her channel her own experiences and insights into this book has been a privilege. For anyone seeking not only to understand the fundamentals of real estate investment but also to be inspired by someone who really cares about their journey, this book is a treasure!

— With heartfelt admiration and love,
Angela Lee Loy, Chairman Aegis Business Solutions Limited

Over the last 16+ years, I have witnessed many people benefiting from Joan Hing King's incredible knowledge in the Real Estate Market. She always thinks outside the box and doesn't take no for an answer! She wears her heart on her sleeve and helps everyone she can! This fabulous book outlines exactly what deals she has done, to build a family legacy in Real Estate!! She leads by example, demonstrating dedication and generosity as she helps everyone. I have learned so much from her by referring friends and family and witnessing all the people that she has helped to get into the Real Estate Market. I am so honoured to endorse this fabulous book. Joan Hing King has taught me and many others how to build wealth in Real Estate. She never judges anyone, as you will see in this priceless book!" Thank you Joan for all your lessons xx

— Joanna Blackmore,
Founder, Blackmore Levy Group

"The Path to Real Estate Riches" demonstrates the value of being prepared to take advantage of investment opportunities when they arise. Joan Hing King keeps the reader engaged, and provides the necessary knowledge to start on your journey to making successful investments.

— Judy O'Beirn,
President Hasmark Publishing International

THE PATH TO REAL ESTATE RICHES

A BEGINNER'S GUIDE TO CREATING YOUR FORTUNE THROUGH PROPERTY INVESTMENT

JOAN HING KING

Hasmark
PUBLISHING
INTERNATIONAL

Hasmark
PUBLISHING
INTERNATIONAL

To my precious children and grandchildren,
Whose laughter and love fill my world,
This book is a tribute to your light,
Forever shining in my heart.

ACKNOWLEDGEMENTS

I am deeply grateful to everyone who played a part in bringing this book to life. My heartfelt appreciation goes to my sister, Angela Lee Loy, for her unwavering support and encouragement.

My deepest thanks to my mentor, Peggy McColl, whose wisdom and guidance shaped the narrative. Special thanks to the team at Hasmark Publishing International, from my dedicated editor, to all the invaluable insights and guidance they provided me with.

To my family, friends, and all who stood by me during late nights of writing, your encouragement kept me going. This book is a testament to the power of collaboration and support.

FOREWORD

*G*reetings, dear readers,

As someone deeply committed to empowering lives through words and wisdom, I am thrilled to introduce you to a book that can genuinely alter the trajectory of your financial destiny: *The Path to Real Estate Riches: A Beginner's Guide to Creating Your Fortune Through Property Investment*.

Real estate has long been regarded as a cornerstone of serious wealth-building strategies. With the ever-increasing fluctuations in economies and markets, the need for a stable investment channel is greater than ever. This book, penned by the astute realtor and investor Joan Hing King, serves as a rich repository of insights drawn from both professional expertise and personal experience.

The beauty of real estate, as Joan keenly notes, is its tangible, intrinsic value. This is not a field of abstract numbers and fluctuating stocks; it is a realm of brick and mortar, of homes and communities, and—most importantly—of people.

What sets this book apart from others in its genre is its accessibility. Joan's writing is approachable and her advice, actionable. Whether you're new to property investment or you simply want to refine your strategy, you'll find tips and tactics here that will make a tangible difference in your investment outcomes.

As a student and teacher of success principles, I can affirm that the road to riches—be it in real estate or any other venture—requires more than just technical know-how. It demands a certain mindset, a specific set of skills, and the right attitudes to navigate the ups and downs that inevitably occur along the way. In this book, Joan goes beyond the "what" and the "how" to also explore the "why," thus providing a holistic approach to real estate investment.

If you're reading these words, you're on the threshold of a potentially life-altering journey. But, like any path, the path to real estate riches requires more than just knowing the route. It requires walking it. So, I invite you—no, I urge you—to dive deeply into the pages that follow. Study them, apply them, and if you feel inclined, let them guide you toward creating your own real estate riches.

To your future success,

Peggy McColl
New York Times best-selling author
Empowering Millions Through Words and Wisdom
http://PeggyMcColl.com <http://peggymccoll.com/>

> *Real estate cannot be lost or stolen, nor can it be carried away. Purchased with common sense, paid for in full, and managed with reasonable care, it is about the safest investment in the world.*
>
> **Franklin D. Roosevelt**

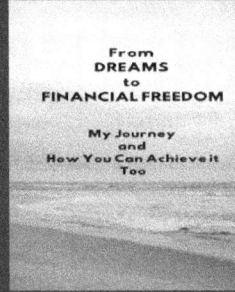

From
DREAMS
to
FINANCIAL FREEDOM

My Journey
and
How You Can Achieve it
Too

Welcome to your guide to real estate investing, where you'll learn the strategies and techniques that I've used to achieve my goal of becoming a successful real estate investor and that have helped me and others to fund the perfect lifestyle now and in retirement. When I started out in real estate investing, I had no idea where to begin and knew nothing about real estate investing; I wasn't a realtor then. I knew I had to educate myself, but since I had three children under the age of 14 and so no money to spare, I chose to do so by means of books and YouTube videos. Between the cost of the children's activities, mortgage payments, food, utilities, etc., I never thought I'd be able to invest in real estate. I certainly didn't have a down payment.

Today, I'm a real estate investor and agent with over 20 years of experience in the industry. I've gained a passion for real estate and a deep understanding of the market, and I've seen it all, from market booms to crashes, and learned valuable lessons along the way. I built up a nest egg by implementing a variety of investment strategies, including "buy and hold," "fix and flip," lease options, sandwich lease options, and commercial syndication.

In this book, you'll gain insights into the different types of real estate investing, the pros and cons of each strategy, and the key factors to consider when making investment decisions. As a beginner investor, you'll gain from this book the knowledge and tools you need to succeed in the world of real estate investing. So let's dive in!

Before we do, however, let's address the elephant in the room: you may have a fear of investing in real estate and therefore choose to continue to rent instead. You may ask, "Can I become wealthy as a real estate investor even if I don't own a home and only rent?" Wealth accumulation depends primarily on one's ability to generate income, save and invest wisely, and manage expenses. So, yes, you can become a wealthy investor without ever owning your home or investing in real estate.

By focusing on building a successful career, starting a business, or investing in assets that appreciate in value, you can accumulate wealth over time. Renting a home can actually be an advantage for some people, as it allows for greater flexibility and mobility, which can be beneficial in pursuing career opportunities or relocating to areas with lower living costs.

On the other hand, owning a home can be a valuable long-term investment. Real estate tends to appreciate in value over time, so if you buy a home and hold onto it for several years, it could potentially increase in value and provide you with significant returns when you sell it.

Additionally, owning a home allows you to build home equity over time, which can be used to finance other investments or to fund your retirement.

There's a difference between owning a property and owning shares in a company:

Aspect	Property (Real Estate)	Stocks
Ownership	Direct ownership of the physical property.	Indirect ownership of shares in a company.
Initial Cost	Typically involves a larger upfront investment.	Can be a smaller initial investment, depending on the stock.

Aspect	Property (Real Estate)	Stocks
Diversification	Limited diversification since the investment is focused on one property.	Greater potential for diversification by investing in multiple stocks.
Leverage	Potential to use leverage through a mortgage.	No leverage provided by the stock investment itself.
Income	Potential rental income from tenants.	Dividends (if the stocks pay dividends) and capital gains from stock appreciation.
Liquidity	Real estate can be relatively illiquid and may take time to sell.	Stocks are generally more liquid and can be bought or sold quickly on the stock market.

Aspect	Property (Real Estate)	Stocks
Risk	Property values can fluctuate but are usually less volatile than stock prices.	Stock prices can be highly volatile and subject to market risks.
Maintenance	Requires ongoing maintenance, repairs, and management.	No direct responsibility for property maintenance.
Tax Benefits	Potential tax deductions such as mortgage interest and property taxes.	Tax advantages such as capital gains tax treatment and qualified dividend tax rates.
Financing	Financing options available, such as mortgages.	Can use stocks as collateral for loans or margin accounts.

It's important to consider these factors and weigh them based on your specific circumstances and investment goals. Both real estate and stocks have their own advantages and risks, and it's advisable to seek professional advice or conduct thorough research before making any investment decisions.

Ultimately, whether you should rent or buy a home depends on your personal financial situation, goals, and priorities. If you're focused on building wealth over the long-term, it may be worth considering homeownership as a viable option.

MYTH-UNDERSTANDINGS

Myth 1: I can't do it.

The truth: If you don't try, you're limiting your potential; until you're fully informed and/or have a coach to help you, you can't know what you can or can't do.

Myth 2: It's too risky; I'll lose money.

The truth: Risk is in direct proportion to how well you hold your incremental costs accountable to producing incremental results; gambling is risky, investing isn't.

Myth 3: I have no money to invest, so there's no point in thinking about investing.

The truth: There are ways in which you can invest with little or no money down.

Myth 4: It would take too much time and effort. I don't have that much time to do research.

The truth: If you knew that, investing only one or two hours a day, you could have financial well-being and then build a portfolio that would provide your family financial invincibility, wouldn't you do it?

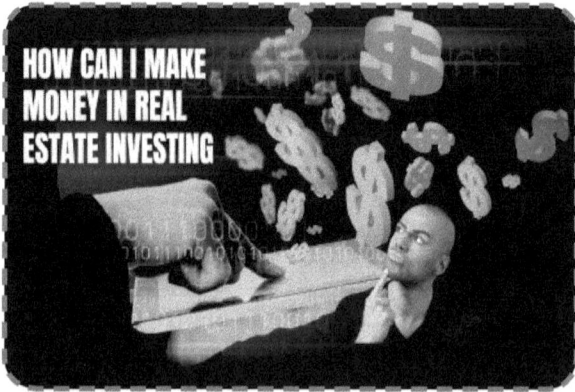

At one point, real estate investing was just a wish of mine, not something I seriously intended to do. However, I began reading real estate investing books such as:

1. *Nothing Down*, by Robert G. Allen;
2. *Rich Dad, Poor Dad*, by Robert Kiyosakiand Sharon Lechter; and
3. *97 Tips for Canadian Real Estate Investors*, by Don R. Campbell.

These were the first three books I read. I went on to read many more.

HOW I STARTED INVESTING IN REAL ESTATE

Where do I start?

Many would-be investors can get themselves into a state of analysis paralysis before taking the plunge. My dive into investing, however, occurred unexpectedly. I was at the time one of 10 women who had begun a stock-trading club modeled on the example of the "Beardstown Ladies." A group of ladies from Beardstown, Illinois, they had created a club to invest in the stock market and each contributed a small amount of money to a common pool. We started with $25 a month.

At one of our meetings, a fellow member told me that she needed to rent an apartment for her son in downtown Toronto and could find nothing in reasonably good condition for less than $1,000 a month. However, she added that there were some new preconstruction condos available that were better than the rentals. (Preconstruction condos involve buying a property from plans.) I trotted off with her to look at the condos. I intended to buy only a one-bedroom condo but decided to buy a studio, as well. I asked the mortgage agent on site whether I could buy two, and she asked how much rent I could get for the units. I told her the rent amounts my friend had provided me, and she told me I could buy both units.

After completing the offer to purchase, I experienced a bout of buyer's remorse, a common feeling after a purchase involving a sizable investment of funds. I went home and asked my husband whether we should give back one of the units. He replied, "If we can't afford both, we'll sell one to pay for the other." Now that we'd got past the buyer's remorse, the next challenge was how to get the down payment.

This was in 1999, and the total for both condos was $160,000–the one-bedroom was $95,000, and the studio was $65,000. I had to come up with a 5% down payment: $8,000. You may laugh at how ridiculous the price was back then, but to us, that was a lot of money. We didn't have even $5,000, much less $8,000.

Lesson 1: When you have a burning desire (read Napoleon Hill's *Think and Grow Rich*), the Universe sends messages in the form of ideas and intuition, and your creative juices start flowing.

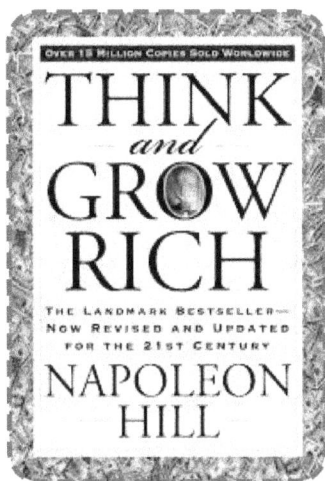

I put on my thinking cap and came up with an idea. I realized that I had a car (a Toyota Corolla) that I could trade in for cash. Toyota offered me $10,000 for the trade-in, and I struck a deal whereby they would buy my car and keep $2,000 as a deposit toward my leasing another Corolla. My lease was only $210 a month for five years, and voila! I now had the $8,000 for the deposit on the condos.

The condos took four years to build, and by that time, my husband and I had saved some money and our salaries had increased. We didn't have to pay any more than the 5% down, but we also needed funds for closing and other ancillary costs. I had a great realtor, and she rented both the studio and one-bedroom as soon as we took possession. Our cash flow from the condos was $500 from the studio and $600 from the one-bedroom.

ATTEND INVESTMENT CLUB MEETINGS

INCREASE YOUR NETWORTH BY INCREASING YOUR NETWORK

Increase your network to increase your net worth.

After doing my first deal, I was hooked on real estate investing. However, none of my friends was in real estate investing, so my next step was finding other investors to network with and learn from.

I decided to become serious about real estate investing and started attending real estate courses. The problem was that I would attend these courses on Saturday and Sunday and come away filled with information, excited and motivated, but when Monday came, I was no further ahead in my investing because there was no one to help me follow through. In addition, most of these courses were taught by Americans, who by Monday had flown back home.

The burning desire to learn more led me to join a real estate club. Unfortunately, that club disbanded after three months because the leaders were all about themselves rather than the members. The three die-hard members who remained were two of my friends and I. When the more experienced of my two friends said he would like to start a club, I volunteered to create a real estate club that included the three of us. I had the names and emails of the attendees of all the courses I'd attended, so I sent an email to about 250 people—and was amazed and surprised when 40 people showed up at the first meeting of the club, all just as eager and motivated to get involved in real estate investing. I ran the Oakville Real Estate Club for 20 years. My goal was to educate, inspire, and help others. When the COVID-19 pandemic began, I stopped the meetings, but you can find "Oakville Real Estate Club" on the social media platform Meetup.

Lesson 2: Stay close to the fire.

I believe that if I had never started this club, I wouldn't have stayed in real estate investing because you must stay "close to the fire" to keep you interested and to learn more from others. This is another recommendation for a new investor. To keep learning and meeting other investors, I recommend that you visit as many real estate investment clubs as possible, as the members can help you with advice, and also with capital when you're ready to partner or share your real estate deals. At our meetings, I would have guest experts such as lawyers, accountants, developers, builders, paralegals, home inspectors, and real estate agents who had investment deals. Real estate investors are very generous with their knowledge and willingness to help other investors—whether new or experienced—build their real estate portfolio.

RESEARCH

*O*ne of the best bits of advice I have received was from a friend who also ran her own real estate investment club. She told me that if I was serious about being a real estate investor, I should spend at least an hour or two every day researching the market.

You don't have to do all of the research I list below; this is my in-depth research. If you understand and actually do Numbers 1 to 6, I think you can start your investing journey.

If you can do only the bare minimum of research as a first-time real estate investor, here are the key areas to focus on:

1. **Location:** Research the local market and identify areas with potential for growth, stability, or high demand.

2. **Economic Factors:** Assess the economic health of the region, including job growth, population trends, and major industries.

3. **Rental Market:** Analyze rental rates, vacancy rates, and rental demand in the area to evaluate the potential rental income.

4. **Property Types:** Determine the type of property you want to invest in (residential, commercial, multi-family, etc.) and evaluate its pros and cons.

5. **Property Condition:** Inspect the property thoroughly to assess its overall condition, identify any necessary repairs or renovations, and estimate associated costs. You can pay a professional to carry out a complete inspection.

6. **Comparable Sales:** Research recent sales of similar properties in the area to determine the property's market value and the potential return on investment. There are many types of apps available that you can use, such as House Sigma.

7. **Financing and Cash Flow:** Explore different financing methods, such as mortgages, loans, or partnerships, and evaluate the associated costs, interest rates, and terms.

8. **Cash Flow Analysis:** Calculate the potential income and expenses related to the property, including mortgage payments, property taxes, insurance, maintenance costs, and vacancy rates. Assess the property's cash flow and profitability.

9. **Legal Considerations:**

   a. *Local Laws and Regulations*: Familiarize yourself with local zoning laws, building codes, rental regulations, and any other legal requirements that may affect your investment.

   b. *Title Search*: Conduct a title search to ensure there are no outstanding liens, encumbrances, or legal issues with the property.

   c. *Contracts and Documentation*: Review and make sure you understand all contracts, agreements, leases, and legal documents involved in the transaction.

10. **Risk Assessment:**

   a. *Property Risks*: Identify potential risks associated with the property, such as environmental hazards, natural disasters, or structural issues.

   b. *Market Risks*: Assess market fluctuations, potential downturns, and the overall stability of the real estate market.

   c. *Financial Risks*: Evaluate your financial capacity to withstand potential losses, consider insurance options, and have contingency plans in place.

11. **Professional Guidance:**

    a. *Real Estate Professionals*: Seek advice from real estate agents, brokers, property managers, or other professionals with expertise in the local market.

    b. *Network*: Connect with local investors or real estate investment groups to gain insights and learn from their experiences.

When you've done your research on these areas, you can set off on your real estate investment journey with the basic knowledge you need to make informed decisions. This is a simplified approach, however; conducting more research and seeking professional guidance will enhance your chances of success. Your next step is to find out about matters of finance.

FINANCE MATTERS

*O*ne of the most important components of real estate investing is qualifying for a mortgage. Here's some useful information to help you understand what lenders are looking for in order to qualify you for a mortgage.

1. Make sure to pay your bills on time and don't have your credit cards and lines of credit maxed out. A credit score of 700 or higher is considered good on the FICO scoring model. However, it's important to note that different mortgage lenders have different criteria and may have varying requirements. Having a good credit score demonstrates to lenders that you have a history of responsible borrowing and are likely to repay your mortgage on time. This can increase your chances of being approved for a mortgage and may qualify you for better loan options.

2. A high credit score is only one of the factors lenders consider when evaluating a mortgage application.

You'll also need to have a good income and debt-to-income ratio, a solid employment history, a down payment, and overall financial stability.

3. **Income and Employment:** Lenders will assess your income stability and employment history to ensure that you have the financial means to repay the mortgage. This means that you'll need to provide documents such as employment letters, pay stubs, and income tax returns.

4. **Credit History:** Your credit history plays a crucial role in mortgage approval. Lenders will review your credit score and credit report to assess your creditworthiness and past payment history.

5. **Down Payment:** You'll typically need to make a down payment toward the purchase price of the home. The minimum required down payment varies depending on the purchase price and the type of mortgage, but it generally ranges from 5% to 20% of the property's value.

6. **Debt-to-Income Ratio:** Lenders analyze your debt-to-income ratio, which is the percentage of your gross monthly income (before taxes) that goes toward payments for rent, mortgage, credit cards, or other debt. A debt-to-credit ratio of 30% or lower is the acceptable

to lenders. If your ratio is higher than 30, lenders may consider that you are a risk and may have problems with paying back the loan. Having a lower ratio is preferred, as it demonstrates your ability to manage debt alongside mortgage payments.

7. **Employment Stability:** Lenders prefer borrowers who have a steady job and a stable income stream.

8. **Property Appraisal:** The lender may require a professional appraisal of the property to determine its market value. This valuation helps in assessing the loan-to-value ratio, which is the mortgage amount compared to the property's appraised value.

9. **Mortgage Insurance:** If your down payment is less than 20% of the property's value, you'll likely need to obtain mortgage insurance from a mortgage insurer approved by the Canadian government. This insurance protects the lender in the event that you default on the mortgage.

10. **Documentation:** You'll need to provide various documents, including identification (such as passport or driver's licence), proof of income, bank statements, and information about the property you're purchasing.

A mortgage is one way to finance the purchase of a property. Here's a list of other financing methods you may want to explore:

1. **Mortgage Financing:** Obtaining a mortgage loan from a bank or a mortgage broker is a common way to finance real estate investments. You can use the property you're purchasing as collateral, and the loan is typically repaid over a fixed term with regular payments.

2. **Home Equity Line of Credit (HELOC):** If you already own a property with equity, you can apply for a HELOC. It allows you to borrow against the equity in your property and use the funds for real estate investments. HELOCs provide flexibility, as you can access the funds as needed and pay interest only on the amount borrowed.

3. **Private Financing:** Private lenders or individual investors may offer financing options, especially for real estate investments that may not meet traditional bank criteria. Private financing can provide more flexibility in terms and conditions but may come with higher interest rates.

4. **Joint Venture (JV) Partnerships:** In a joint venture, you collaborate with another investor or company to pool financial resources and expertise. This

arrangement can help you access financing and share the risks and rewards of the investment.

5. **Vendor Take-Back Mortgage (VTB):** In some cases, the property seller may be willing to finance part of the purchase by creating a VTB. This involves the seller acting as the lender and providing a mortgage to the buyer. The vendor continues to own a percentage of the home equal to the amount of the loan until it's been paid. This can be beneficial if traditional financing is not available or if you negotiate favourable terms with the seller.

6. **Self-Directed Registered Retirement Savings Plan (RRSP):** If you have funds in an RRSP, you can use them to invest in real estate. The Canadian government's Home Buyers' Plan (HBP) lets you withdraw funds from your RRSP to buy or build a home for yourself (or for a relative with a disability) and pay the funds back over 15 years. There's no withholding tax on amounts of $35,000 or less. (Note that there are certain RRSPs—locked-in or group RRSPs, for example—from which you can't withdraw funds.)

After you've done your research on the location, you need to determine how much money you have (or don't have) to start investing in real estate. First, figure out which strategy is best suited to you. Here are some you can consider.

BIRD-DOGGING

*B*ird-dogging is a term commonly used in real estate investing to describe the act of locating properties with investment potential and passing the information on to real estate investors in exchange for a fee or a share of the profits. The bird dog, also known as a property scout, essentially acts as a middleman between sellers and investors.

Bird-dogging is legal in Canada. However, it's essential to understand that specific regulations and licensing requirements may vary by province or territory. It's best to consult with a local real estate professional or lawyer to make sure you comply with the laws and regulations in your area.

In general, bird-dogging involves finding and identifying potential investment properties and then referring them to real estate investors or other professionals. As long as you aren't engaging in activities that require a real estate licence, such as negotiating or facilitating the sale of properties on behalf of others, bird-dogging is typically considered permissible.

Bird-dogging is one way to get into real estate investing using sweat equity rather than the bank's money. You'll learn a lot while scouting and make money at the same time.

Advantages of Bird-Dogging:

1. **Low Financial Risk:** Bird-dogging doesn't require a significant amount of capital to get started. As a property scout, you're essentially using your knowledge and time to find potential deals, rather than investing your own money.

2. **Learning Opportunities:** Bird-dogging can be an excellent way to gain practical experience in real estate investing without the financial risks associated with being a full-fledged investor. You can learn about different neighbourhoods, property values, and the overall process of real estate transactions.

3. **Networking:** As a bird dog, you'll interact with various real estate professionals, including investors, real estate agents, and property owners. This provides an opportunity to build a network of contacts within the industry, which can be beneficial for future endeavours.

4. **Extra Income:** If you're able to find and present lucrative deals to investors, you can earn a fee or a percentage of the profit when the deal is successfully closed. Bird-dogging can be a way to generate additional income, especially if you have a knack for finding good investment opportunities.

Disadvantages of Bird-Dogging:

1. **Income Uncertainty:** Since bird-dogging requires you to find and refer properties to investors, your income can be uncertain. If you're unable to find profitable deals consistently or if the investors you work with don't close on the deals, your earnings are likely to be limited.

2. **Lack of Control:** As a bird dog, you aren't directly involved in the decision-making or the execution of the real estate deals. The investors have the final say on whether to pursue a property, and you have limited control over the outcome.

3. **Competitive Market:** In many real estate markets, bird-dogging can be a competitive field. Other property scouts are also looking for deals, and it can be challenging to find unique opportunities that haven't already been discovered by others.

4. **Limited Long-Term Gains:** While bird-dogging can provide some immediate income, it may not offer the same long-term financial benefits as becoming an active real estate investor. As a bird dog, you're essentially trading your time for a fee, rather than building your own portfolio and generating passive income.

I've never done bird-dogging myself, but I did get a deal from a bird dog—a bungalow about one hour from where I lived.

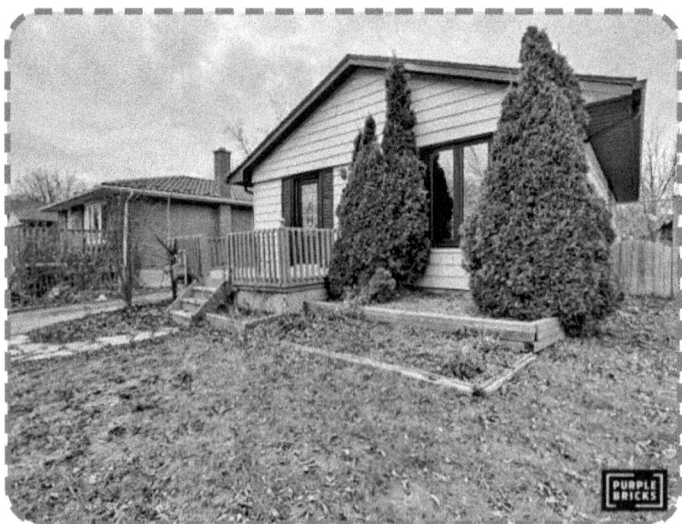

I had a home inspection done, and since there were only minor problems, I bought the house. I received total rents of $2,300 a month as follows:

Basement: $850
Main floor: $900
Bachelor unit: $550

Total rent: $2,300 less mortgage and expenses of $1,300 = $1,000 profit

The cash flow of $1,000 made it an attractive buy.

Buy and Hold (My Goldmine)

Buy and hold is a real estate investment strategy in which an investor purchases a property with the intention of holding onto it for an extended period of time, typically several years or even decades. The investor aims to generate income from the property through rental payments and to potentially benefit from long-term appreciation in the property's value.

Advantages of Buy and Hold

1. **Steady cash flow:** By renting out the property to tenants, investors can generate regular rental income, which can provide a consistent cash flow stream over time.

2. **Long-term appreciation:** Real estate has the potential to increase in value over the long term. By holding onto a property for an extended period, investors can benefit from appreciation, which can lead to significant gains when the property is eventually sold.

3. **Tax advantages:** Real estate investors can take advantage of various tax benefits, such as depreciation deductions, which can reduce taxable income and potentially increase overall returns.

4. **Equity buildup:** As the investor pays down the mortgage over time, the equity in the property increases. This can provide opportunities for future refinancing or accessing equity for other investment purposes.

5. **Leverage:** Real estate allows investors to use leverage by financing a portion of the purchase price through a mortgage. This can amplify returns and increase the potential for higher profits.

Disadvantages

1. **Capital tie-up:** Investing in real estate typically requires a significant amount of capital, which can limit diversification and tie up funds for an extended

period. Liquidity can be a challenge if the investor needs to sell the property quickly.

2. **Property management responsibilities:** Owning and managing rental properties involves various responsibilities, such as finding tenants, dealing with maintenance and repairs, and handling tenant issues. This requires time, effort, and potentially additional costs for property management services.

3. **Market risk:** Real estate values can fluctuate based on market conditions. While long-term appreciation is a common expectation, there can be periods of stagnant or declining property values, which may affect overall returns.

4. **Economic factors:** The profitability of a buy-and-hold strategy can be influenced by economic factors such as interest rates, unemployment rates, and local market conditions. Economic downturns or unfavourable conditions in a particular area can affect rental demand and property values.

5. **Regulatory and legal considerations:** Real estate investing is subject to various regulations and legal requirements. Investors need to stay informed about local laws, zoning regulations, landlord-tenant laws, and other legal considerations to ensure compliance and mitigate potential risks.

My Story

I call this property "my goldmine." I bought it when my husband was given early retirement and I was starting my career as a real estate agent. Needless to say, we wouldn't qualify for a mortgage. This property was $217,000 and I had to come up with 25% down, or $50,000. I had my last $50,000 in my RRSP (we lost over $400,000 in RRSP savings when we were in business after my husband retired). Both my children were in retail jobs, not making that much, but together, they made enough to qualify for the mortgage. I gifted them the $50,000 for the down payment. (Some lenders may require that the gift come from a family member, while others may allow gifts from friends.)

Lesson 3: Don't pay off all your debts; create assets. This is a lesson I learned from reading the book *The Millionaire Maker*, by Loral Langemeier.

I call this property my goldmine because after I bought it in 2004, the equity appreciation went up one year later by $85,000 more than the amount I paid for it. With this new-found equity, I went to the bank and asked for a $50,000 line of credit–in essence, I had put no money down. I took the $50,000 that the bank gave me and invested it in another property. That property is in one of the best areas in Toronto, and it appreciates every year. Today it's worth more than $1,000,000.

My goldmine is the only property I wouldn't sell unless I had to. The title of the property is still in my kids' names, and we've decided this will be our safe home–our refuge if anything happens.

Fix and Flip

Advantages of Fix and Flip

1. **Profit Potential:** By purchasing a property at a discounted price, making improvements, and then selling it at a higher value, investors can earn a significant return on their investment. The primary advantage of fix and flip is the potential for substantial profits.

2. **Active Income:** Fix-and-flip investing provides an opportunity for active income generation. Investors can actively participate in the renovation process, overseeing the improvements and increasing the property's value through their efforts.

3. **Control:** Fix-and-flip investors have control over various aspects of the investment. They can choose the property they want to purchase, decide on the extent of renovations, and determine the selling price and the marketing strategy.

4. **Real Estate Market Knowledge:** Engaging in fix-and-flip projects allows investors to gain valuable knowledge about the real estate market. They become familiar with property values, market trends, and renovation costs, which can be beneficial for future investments.

My Story

In 2005, I became a realtor and at an open house met an investor who wanted to buy a property that I had listed. Unfortunately, the investor had no money and bad credit. However, he said he had a friend who had the credit but not the down payment. I decided to find the down payment for them.

The friend wanted me to guarantee them that they would make a profit after the property was sold. I said,

"Let me understand this: I am going to get you the down payment, it's my listing (I'll get a commission), and you want a guarantee that you will make a profit?" There and then, I decided to become the investor's partner and that's how I got into fix and flip.

The deal went like this. I created a lease for the property, as the investor partner/renovator would be staying in the house while he fixed it up. The bank approved the mortgage because I had a lease in place and I had already borrowed the 25% down payment (this was the requirement at the time).

Lesson 4: Never give away a deal until you've explored all the possibilities and are certain that you aren't able to benefit from the deal.

Syndication

Syndication in real estate investment refers to the process of pooling capital and resources from multiple investors to invest collectively in a real estate project. It involves the formation of a syndicate or partnership, typically led by a sponsor, or syndicator, who is responsible for identifying, acquiring, and managing the investment property.

Advantages of Syndication:

1. **Access to Larger Investments:** Syndication allows individual investors to participate in larger and more lucrative real estate deals that may have been unattainable on their own. By pooling resources, investors can collectively acquire properties with higher value, potential returns, and growth opportunities.

2. **Diversification:** Real estate syndication enables investors to diversify their portfolios across different properties, locations, and asset classes. This diversification helps mitigate risk by reducing exposure to a single property or market, as investments are spread across a portfolio of properties.

3. **Professional Expertise:** Syndication allows investors to leverage the expertise and experience of the syndicator or sponsor who is responsible for the day-to-day management of the investment. These

professionals have specialized knowledge in acquiring, managing, and optimizing real estate assets, which can potentially lead to better investment outcomes.

4. **Limited Liability:** Investors in real estate syndication typically have limited liability, meaning that their personal assets are protected from the liabilities and debts of the investment. This provides a level of risk mitigation and shields individual investors from potential financial losses beyond their initial investment.

Disadvantages of Syndication:

1. **Limited Control:** Syndication involves a collective decision-making process, and individual investors may have limited control over the management and operation of the investment property. Key decisions are often made by the syndicator or sponsor, potentially leaving some investors with less influence over the direction of the investment.

2. **Potential Lack of Liquidity:** Real estate investments are generally illiquid, meaning that they can't be easily converted to cash. Syndicated investments often come with lock-up periods—that is, investors are committed to a specific holding period. This lack of liquidity can limit an investor's ability to access his or her capital quickly.

3. **Distribution of Profits:** Syndication structures involve the distribution of profits among multiple investors. While this allows for diversification, it also means that returns are split among the syndicate members, reducing the potential profit for each, compared to a standalone investment.

My Story

Investing in a syndication requires a high level of trust and transparency between the syndicator and investors. It's crucial for investors to thoroughly vet the syndicator's track record, communication practices, and investment strategies to ensure that interests are aligned and to minimize the risk of potential conflicts. I was able to attract my investors because they all knew me and trusted me.

As with all my learning about these strategies, my experience with syndication came about as a result of the opportunities coming to me and my ability to figure out whether a given deal was one I should take on or give away. This opportunity presented itself through my activity as a realtor.

My client had two offers on two "Live/Work" properties (these are properties with four levels; the top two levels are the residential part of the property, and the commercial part is on the ground floor and in the basement). My client decided that she wanted only one of them. The unit she didn't want was, I felt, the better of the two, and I really wanted to buy it, as it was a corner unit and I could see the potential. These Live/Work units were no longer going to be built in this particular town, as there was no more land on which to build a unit where someone had options: live there and carry on a business, live there and rent out the commercial part, or rent out both the residential and commercial parts of the building.

However, I had the usual problem: I didn't have the money, and, of course, I didn't have the down payment. After much thinking, I decided to form a syndication and asked five of my friends if they would like to invest in this property with me. They all accepted my offer.

I consulted a lawyer, and he created a joint venture agreement and incorporated a company. One of the great things about this deal is that one of the investors was a husband and wife team who were financially solid and able to be approved for the mortgage on their own. The lawyer set up the deal as follows.

The couple-investors were the first directors of the corporation, and all the other investors were shareholders. We all had one share for $1.00 each. The lawyer also created a shareholders' agreement that included all the terms and conditions. We easily rented the residential and commercial units quickly, as the building was on a busy street with lots of pedestrians—being a corner unit with lots of windows, it was ideal for attracting business. Throughout the time we held the property, there were no problems, and we had a property manager who looked after repairs and maintenance. When one shareholder backed out, we were easily able to fill the position because it was such a lucrative and therefore desirable investment.

RENT TO OWN

A rent-to-own strategy is a real estate arrangement whereby a tenant rents a property for a set period of time with an option to purchase the property at a later date, usually within three to five years. This option is typically exercised by paying a predetermined price to the landlord at the end of the rental period. In essence, the structure of a rent-to-own has two parts: first, a usual rental with conditions, and second, when the tenant decides to own, it becomes a regular offer to purchase.

Here's how it works:

1. The tenant and landlord agree to a rental period and a purchase price for the property.

2. The tenant pays an upfront option fee, typically between 1% and 5% of the purchase price. This fee gives the tenant the right to purchase the property at the end of the rental period. The option fee is

credited to the tenant when she or he purchases the property.

3. The tenant pays rent as usual, but a portion of the rent is credited toward the purchase price of the property. This credit is usually between 10% and 20% above the monthly rent. These credits are given to the tenant when she or he purchases the property.

4. At the end of the rental period, the tenant can choose to exercise the option to purchase the property by paying the predetermined purchase price.

5. If the tenant decides not to exercise the option, she or he forfeits the option fee and the rent credits. The property remains the landlord's, and the tenant moves out.

This strategy can be attractive to tenants who want to become homeowners but may not have the savings or credit score to obtain a mortgage loan immediately. It can also be beneficial for landlords who are having trouble finding buyers for their properties.

However, both parties should carefully consider the terms of the agreement, as there may be risks and potential drawbacks involved. It's important to have a clear understanding of the contract and to consult with a real estate attorney to ensure that both parties' rights and interests are protected.

Advantages of Rent to Own (RTO):

1. **No need for a large upfront payment:** Rent to own allows individual buyers to acquire a property without a significant initial down payment. This can be advantageous for those who may not have the funds available immediately.

2. **Potential for eventual ownership:** One of the primary benefits of RTO is the possibility of owning the property in the future. Rent payments typically go toward building equity, and there's an opportunity to convert the rental agreement into full ownership over time.

3. **Time to improve creditworthiness:** Rent-to-own arrangements can be suitable for those with less-than-perfect credit scores. Renting the property initially provides an opportunity to improve creditworthiness over time, making it easier to secure a mortgage or financing for the purchase later.

4. **Test before committing:** Renting a property before purchasing allows potential buyers to assess whether it meets their needs and preferences. This "trial period" enables them to gauge the property's

suitability, functionality, and compatibility with their lifestyle.

Disadvantages of Rent to Own (RTO):

1. **Higher overall cost:** The total cost of acquiring a property through a rent-to-own agreement is often higher than the cost of purchasing it outright. Rent payments typically include a premium that goes toward building equity, and this added cost can accumulate over time.

2. **Limited control during the rental phase:** While renting, the potential buyer may have limited control over the property. Certain modifications or changes may require the owner's approval, and the renter might not have the freedom to make alterations according to his or her preferences.

3. **Risk of forfeiting invested funds:** If the tenant fails to meet the terms of the rent-to-own agreement, he or she may risk forfeiting the equity built through rent payments. Any missed payments or breaches of the agreement's terms could result in losing the opportunity to purchase the property.

4. **Less flexibility to change plans:** Committing to a rent-to-own agreement means having less flexibility to change plans or move to a different location. If circumstances change or if the tenant/buyer decides

that he or she no longer wants to pursue ownership, he or she might have trouble terminating the agreement without financial consequences.

It's crucial to evaluate personal circumstances thoroughly and to review the terms and conditions of any rent-to-own agreement carefully to determine if it aligns with individual goals and financial capabilities. Consulting with a real estate or legal professional can provide further guidance and help in making an informed decision.

Structuring a rent-to-own agreement involves several key components that need to be considered. Here's a step-by-step guide on how to structure a rent-to-own arrangement:

1. **Define the terms:** Determine the specific terms of the agreement, including the duration of the rental period, the purchase price of the property, and the portion of the monthly rent that will be credited toward the eventual purchase.

2. **Establish the option fee:** The option fee, also known as the upfront fee, is a non-refundable payment made by the tenant to secure the option to purchase the property at a later date. This fee is typically separate from the security deposit and is negotiable between the parties involved.

3. **Set the purchase price:** Determine what the purchase price of the property will be at the end of the rental period. This can be a fixed price agreed upon upfront or can be based on an appraisal at the time of purchase. Ensure that the purchase price is fair and reasonable for both parties.

4. **Determine the rental payment structure:** Decide on the monthly rental amount, taking into account such factors as market rent, the portion that will be credited toward the purchase, and any additional fees or charges. Clearly outline the payment due dates and the consequences of late or missed payments. The monthly payment is usually market rent plus an amount over and above the monthly rent.

5. **Specify the maintenance and repairs responsibilities:** Define the responsibilities for maintenance and repairs during the rental period. Typically, the landlord retains responsibility for major repairs, while the tenant is responsible for routine maintenance and minor repairs.

6. **Include an option period:** Define the duration of the option period—the timeframe during which the tenant has the right to purchase the property. This period can range from several months to a few years, depending on the agreement.

7. **Outline the conditions for purchase:** Specify the conditions that must be met for the tenant to exercise her or his option to purchase. These may include such factors as a minimum credit score, proof of stable income, or the absence of any legal disputes. Usually, the tenant/buyer would use this period to fix her or his credit. A good seller/landlord would make sure to check that the tenant/buyer is working on her or his credit so that when it comes time to buy, the tenant/buyer will quality for a mortgage.

8. **Address default and termination clauses:** Clearly state the consequences of a default such as missed payments or breach of the agreement's terms. Outline the process for resolving disputes and the conditions for terminating the agreement.

9. **Consult legal and financial professionals:** Experts recommend strongly that you seek legal and financial advice when structuring a rent-to-own agreement. Doing so ensures compliance with local laws, protects the interests of both parties, and helps navigate any complexities or unique circumstances.

At the final closing of a rent-to-own, the seller/landlord refunds the tenant/buyer his or her down payment and all monthly amounts above market rent. Should the tenant/buyer not go through with the rent-to-own, he or she loses whatever monies he or she has put in—the down payment and all amounts above the monthly rent.

My Story

At the beginning of this book, I told the story of how I bought my first two condos when I began my real estate investing career. I later bought a third one, so at one point, I had three condos at the same time, and I wanted to sell one of them because the mortgage payment on the third was higher than for the other two. My reasoning was that if I had vacancies in all of them, I needed to unload one so I could manage the mortgage payments. However, this was early on in my career as an investor and I wasn't yet a real estate agent. Moreover, condo sales in Toronto at the time were slowing down. As always when I have a challenge to sort out, I turn to a book. You can find solutions for almost any challenge in a book; there's always a book that deals with your situation.

I decided to reread one of my favourite real estate books, Robert Allen's *Nothing Down*. When I came across the chapter "Rent to Own," I jumped off my chair. "That's what I'll do," I thought. Being a legal secretary at the time, I understood the concept: a rental with a promise to buy in the future. I found online the forms for creating a rent-to-own. I put an ad in the newspaper, had all my forms ready, and waited for people to attend my open house.

The first person who came in asked for information about the rent-to-own concept because he was thinking of selling his place to his nephew. He ended up buying the condo outright. The second person who walked in was very interested in my documents. Two weeks later, I attended a real estate course and found that this person was giving the course!

Despite selling that condo outright, I did end up becoming a rent-to-own investor with one of my first condos. I wanted to sell my one-bedroom condo but thought I should use the rent-to-own strategy because I'd get more monthly cash flow and a lump sum payment for the option to purchase in three years. I offered the unit for $200,000–that was the going price and I'd already made $100,000-plus in profit since I bought it. The terms for purchase or to exercise the option were that if the tenant exercised the option in three years, the price would increase by 3% of the offer price of $200,000, by 4% after four years, and by 5% after five years.

I had been renting my unit to a chef who never cooked in the condo, washed dishes, or used the microwave, as he was there only to sleep, and the unit was just as I had rented it to him. I put an ad in the local papers.

The first person who came to look at the unit was a young lady in her 30s who had been renting a bachelor/studio unit for nine years. She was overcome by how big the unit was and how new the appliances appeared. The icing on the cake was that there was a parking space available with the unit, and since she didn't drive, she'd be able to rent out the parking space for $100 a month. We agreed on a rent-to-own arrangement.

She was a great tenant, and after three years, she decided to exercise her option. She had put down $3,000 for the option to purchase, and that deposit money was to go back to her when she exercised her option, and she had paid an extra $200 per month, which also went back to her. Here's how I structured the deal when she decided to exercise the option.

One-bedroom unit—bought for $99,000

Rental Unit, rent: $1,200 per month, minus mortgage of $400 = $800 cash flow per month

Rent to Own cash flow first year rental: total cash flow $800 per month + $200 extra cash flow per month = $1,000 per month

Sold unit after three years at $200,000

Profit:

$200K - $99K = $101,000

Rental cash flow = $800 X 12 = $9,600

After Rent to Own cash flow = $800 + $200 = $1,000 X 36 = $36,000

Total Profit = $146,600 (after three years)

Overall I made approximately $146,600, plus I sold my one-bedroom for a $120,000 profit, for a total profit of $266,600 within three years on my first investment—not a bad return from a Toyota Corolla worth $10,000.

SANDWICH LEASE OPTION

A sandwich lease option is a real estate strategy in which an investor leases a property from a seller/owner with the option to buy it, and then subleases it to a tenant/buyer with the option to buy it from the investor. The investor acts as the middleman between the seller and the tenant/buyer.

There are several reasons an investor may want to consider a sandwich lease option:

Advantages:

1. **Limited funds:** If an investor doesn't have enough capital to purchase a property outright, a sandwich lease option allows him or her to control the property without having to make a large initial investment.

2. **Flexibility:** A sandwich lease option can offer more flexibility than traditional real estate transactions because

the terms of the lease and purchase agreement can be negotiated to suit the needs of all parties involved.

3. **Cash flow:** By subleasing the property to a tenant/buyer, the investor can generate cash flow through rental payments and potentially a higher option fee from the tenant/buyer.

4. **Profit potential:** If the investor is able to purchase the property at a lower price than what the tenant/buyer is willing to pay, there's the potential for a profit when the tenant/buyer exercises the option to buy.

It's important to note that sandwich lease options can also come with risks, such as the possibility of the seller backing out of the deal or the tenant/buyer defaulting on payments. It's essential to do thorough research and to have a solid understanding of the real estate market and the legal requirements involved in this strategy before pursuing a sandwich lease option.

Disadvantages

While a sandwich lease option can offer certain advantages, it's important to be aware of the potential disadvantages and risks associated with this real estate strategy:

1. **Limited control:** As the middleman in a sandwich lease option, you may have limited control over

the property. You are still subject to the terms of the original lease with the seller, and if any issues arise between the seller and the tenant/buyer, you may be caught in the middle.

2. **Legal complexities:** Sandwich lease options can involve complex legal agreements and contracts. It's crucial to have a solid understanding of the legal requirements and to consult with an experienced legal professional who knows the strategy to ensure compliance with local laws and regulations.

3. **Financial risks:** If the tenant/buyer defaults on lease payments or decides not to exercise the option to purchase, you may be responsible for covering the costs, including the original lease payments to the seller. This can result in financial losses and added burdens.

4. **Seller cooperation:** The success of a sandwich lease option depends on the cooperation of both the seller and the tenant/buyer. If the seller decides to back out of the agreement or is uncooperative, it can complicate the process and lead to a failed transaction.

5. **Market fluctuations:** Real estate markets can be unpredictable, and if property values decline during the lease term, it may affect the profitability of the

sandwich lease option. You may find it challenging to sell the property to the tenant/buyer at a higher price, potentially resulting in less profit or a loss. Remember that you're investing, not gambling—always look to the end results you want and the possibility that the outcome may not be what you intended. There are ways you can manage every outcome; you just have to reach out to other investors or consult a book. This strategy isn't used by many investors, but because it doesn't require any capital at the outset, it might be worth considering.

6. **Regulatory and ethical considerations:** In some areas, sandwich lease options may be subject to specific regulations or restrictions. It's important to understand the legal and ethical implications of this strategy to ensure compliance and avoid potential legal issues.

It's crucial to research and assess the risks involved thoroughly before entering into a sandwich lease option. It's also advisable to seek advice from professionals, such as a real estate lawyer or experienced investors, to navigate the process and mitigate potential drawbacks.

The worst scenario is that if necessary, you can give the property back to the seller/owner and your loss of capital will be minimal.

My Story

At one of my real estate investment club meetings in 2005, an investor told me that he had just bought two properties from an investment group that had just renovated some old townhouses in a great location, but the group hadn't helped him to rent it out and he wanted my assistance. I was a realtor then, and I agreed to help him. I asked if he was open to a rent-to-own, and he said that he would definitely consider that option. Here's the deal I put together.

These townhouses were originally rentals that an investor (let's call him Investor A) had bought and turned into condos. As an incentive to investors to buy the units, he renovated the units and gave the buyer/investor a $30,000 cash-back. The second investor (Investor B) wasn't happy because the original investor had sold the units but didn't help him rent them out. The going rate for rentals in the area was $1,300 a month, so I told the investor that if he would take $1,200 rent in exchange for my management, I would rent-to-own it from him, the transaction to be completed in three years. Investor B was happy with that because he just wanted to get the property off his hands, as he hadn't any rental income for six months because Investor A, who had been expected to help him, disappeared once he completed the offer to purchase with Investor B.

I took over the properties and in less than a month was able to rent them for $1,395 a month each, giving me a $195 cash flow a month, as I had to pay the investor only $1,200.

Here's how I explain the concept of a sandwich lease option. The seller/Investor B and the tenant are each the top and bottom of the sandwich and I am the middleman, who is between the Seller/Investor A/Optionor and the eventual Tenant/Buyer/Optionee.

Profit:

Management fees from Owner/seller: $150.00

Rent-to-Own Strategy to Increase Monthly Profit: rented unit for $1,400 per month

Annual Cash Flow = $350 X 12 months = $4,200 X 2 units = $8,400

Remember, you have put no money down. You have three to five years to get your credit and down payment to buy the property.

In this scenario, I sold one unity to help buy the other unit.

BUYING PRECONSTRUCTION

*B*uying a condo in preconstruction refers to the process of purchasing a condominium unit before it's built or completed. This means that the development is still in its planning or construction phase, and the buyer is essentially buying the right to own a unit that doesn't yet exist. In other words, you're buying a unit or property from plans.

Here are some key aspects and steps involved in buying a condo in preconstruction:

1. **Developer's Proposal:** Developers announce new condo projects and provide details about the proposed development, including location, amenities, floor plans, pricing, and expected completion date. They often create marketing materials, such as brochures or websites, to attract potential buyers.

2. **Reservation:** Interested buyers can reserve a specific unit by signing a reservation agreement and

paying a reservation deposit. The deposit amount varies, but it's typically a percentage of the total purchase price.

3. **Sales Contract:** Once the developer finalizes the project plans and obtains the necessary approvals, it will prepare a sales contract. This contract outlines the terms and conditions of the purchase, including the purchase price, payment schedule, estimated completion date, condo rules, and any other pertinent details. It's essential to review this contract thoroughly and seek legal advice if necessary before signing.

4. **Deposit Payments:** After signing the sales contract, the buyer is required to make a series of deposit payments according to a predetermined payment schedule. The payment structure varies by developer but typically involves multiple installments over the construction period, with the final payment due upon completion.

5. **Construction Period:** While the construction is underway, the buyer doesn't have immediate access to the property. However, she or he will receive regular updates from the developer regarding the project's progress.

6. **Interim Occupancy:** In some cases, once the building is deemed safe for occupancy, the buyer may be

allowed to move into the unit before the condominium is officially registered. During this interim occupancy period, the buyer typically pays an occupancy fee, which covers the builder's costs, such as interest on construction financing, property taxes, and maintenance fees.

7. **Final Closing:** When the condominium is completed and ready for occupancy, the buyer proceeds to the final closing. At this stage, the buyer pays any remaining balance, including closing costs, land transfer taxes, and legal fees. The developer then transfers ownership of the unit to the buyer through a deed or title.

It's crucial to conduct due diligence, research the developer's track record, review the contract thoroughly, and consider consulting a real estate lawyer or advisor to ensure a smooth and informed buying process.

Advantages:

1. **Lower Initial Cost:** Buying a condo in preconstruction often allows you to secure a lower purchase price than what you'd pay buying a completed unit. Developers may offer promotional pricing or early-bird incentives to attract buyers, providing an opportunity for potential savings.

2. **Customization Options:** Purchasing preconstruction gives you the chance to have input in the design and customization of your unit. You may be able to choose among a selection of finishes, materials, and upgrades, allowing you to personalize your space to your liking.

3. **Potential for Price Appreciation:** As the construction progresses and the development nears completion, there's a possibility that the property's value will increase. If the real estate market in the area is strong, you may benefit from capital appreciation by the time you take possession of the unit.

4. **Newer Amenities and Features:** Preconstruction condos often feature modern amenities, updated building systems, and the latest technology. You may have access to state-of-the-art facilities, such as fitness centres, swimming pools, rooftop gardens, or smart-home integration.

Disadvantages:

1. **Construction Delays:** Construction projects can face unexpected delays due to various factors, such as permit issues, labour shortages, or weather conditions. As a buyer, you should be prepared for potential delays that could postpone your move-in date and disrupt your plans.

2. **Uncertainty in Final Product:** When purchasing a preconstruction condo, you rely on architectural plans and marketing materials to visualize the final product. There may be a level of uncertainty regarding the quality of construction, layout, or finishes until the project is completed.

3. **Changes to Plans:** Developers may make changes to the original plans during the construction process. While these changes are usually minor, they could affect the layout, size, or design of your unit. It's crucial to review your contract to understand the developer's rights to make modifications.

4. **Financial Risks:** There's a level of financial risk associated with buying preconstruction. If the market conditions change unfavourably by the time of completion, the value of your investment could decrease. In addition, there's a risk that the developer may face financial difficulties or fail to complete the project, potentially affecting your purchase.

5. **No Immediate Occupancy:** Buying preconstruction means that you'll have to wait for the construction to be completed before moving into your unit. If you need a place to live immediately, this could be a disadvantage. Interim occupancy periods may be allowed, but it's important to understand the associated fees and limitations.

It's essential to carefully consider these advantages and disadvantages, conduct thorough research, and weigh the risks before deciding to purchase a condo in preconstruction. It's also advisable to consult with professionals, such as real estate agents and lawyers, who can provide guidance based on your specific circumstances.

My Story

In the last six years, I have concentrated only on buying preconstruction, either on my own or in partnership with others. I've found that the deposit structure is a way to put some money down, for example, 10%. This down payment is usually stretched out over a period of one to two years. If it's a condo project, it usually takes about three to four years before it's built and you're allowed to move in at interim occupancy (see "Interim Occupancy" above). Final occupancy–which is when title to the unit is given to you–may take three more months or as many as 12 months.

I concentrated on preconstruction because when the unit was finally built after two years for a house and three to four years for a condo unit, the property would have appreciated, and I typically made 50–100% return on my deposit investment. This kind of return may not be as common today as in recent years, as real estate prices aren't increasing as fast as they did in the past.

Preconstruction Purchases in the Last 6 Years

Eglinton & Yonge, Toronto, 2017

Esplanade, Grimsby, Ont., 2016
Bought with a Friend

Willow Lane, Stoney Creek, Ont., 2018

Ordinance Toronto, 2015
Bought with a Friend

Muskoka Golf & Country, 2017

Waterdown, Ont., 2019

Sommersides, Niagara Falls, Ont., 2020

IN CONCLUSION...

I n this *Beginner's Guide*, we've explored the world of real estate investing and equipped you with the knowledge and tools necessary to embark on a successful journey. Throughout the e-book, we delved into a variety of real estate strategies, ranging from fix-and-flip properties to rental investments and beyond. Understanding the unique characteristics and potential pitfalls of each strategy, you're now equipped to make informed decisions tailored to your goals and circumstances. We also explored the process of getting started and building a strong foundation through education and networking so you can have a clear understanding of the crucial steps needed to begin your real estate journey.

It's worth stressing once again the importance of devoting one or two hours a day to research in real estate investing. Through diligent market analysis, evaluating property values and trends, and conducting due diligence, you can minimize risks and maximize returns.

As you conclude this e-book, remember that real estate investing is a journey that requires dedication, ongoing education, and adaptability. The information and insights I've shared in this guide can help you to move forward, but ultimately it's your passion, persistence, and willingness to learn that will bring you the most success. By harnessing the knowledge gained here and continuously honing your skills, you will undoubtedly achieve your real estate goals and build a prosperous future.

During my own journey, I was lucky (preparation meeting opportunity) enough not to encounter many disastrous challenges, but, as I said before, if you're prepared for what may happen and continue to keep in touch with other experienced investors, as well as with legal and accounting professionals, you'll be able to find solutions for whatever challenges you may face.

Now, go out and apply these principles with confidence, transforming your aspirations into reality in the exciting world of real estate investing.

ABOUT THE AUTHOR

They say experience is the best teacher, and if that's the case, consider Joan Hing King your mentor in mastering the art of real estate investment. With 20 years of hands-on experience in the property market and 15 years as a seasoned realtor, Joan is not just another expert but a proven authority in the field.

A Self-Made Success Story

Starting with zero money and no experience, Joan embarked on a journey to financial freedom—one property at a time. But it wasn't just about buying and selling; it was about learning. Through tireless reading and attending real estate investment courses,

Joan gained the skills and insights that many spend a lifetime acquiring.

A Jack of All Trades

From buy-and-hold strategies to fix-and-flip ventures, from rent-to-own schemes to sandwich lease options, and even diving into the intricate world of syndication, Joan has done it all. If there's a path to wealth through property, you can bet she has walked it—or paved it for others.

Why Should You Listen?

Decades of Experience: Two decades in investment and 15 years in realty isn't just a stint; it's a lifetime of valuable lessons.

Diverse Skill Set: With hands-on experience in a broad array of investment strategies, Joan offers not just depth but breadth of knowledge.

From Zero to Hero: Starting with nothing and rising to a real estate mogul, Joan is the epitome of the self-made success story.

Testimonials

"Having Joan as a guide on my real estate journey was like having a GPS that led me to treasure!" - Emily K., aspiring investor